MW01075539

just GRANDPARENTS

© artwolfe.com, Przewalski's wild horse & foal

For Grandma Bell,
Highly recommended grandmother and hugger.

© Robert Winslow, Alligator

Acknowledgements

Hearty thanks once again to the photographers who
make these books possible. Clearly, I have
the easy part of the job.

Humble thanks to my editor, Andrea Donner,
who is unceasingly pleasant, professional and prolific.

And special thanks to Grandma Betty, Grandpa Fred,
Mimi, Tutu and Pop Pop for eclectic
and unforgettable inspiration.

My life is blessed; I have held my children's children.

Jeremy Taylor (1613 – 1667)
English bishop and theologian

I could never understand why people were so batty over their grandchildren until mine came into my life. Everything *they do, everything they are is precious.*

Sally Stuart
American author

© C.C. Lockwood / Bruce Coleman, Inc., Alligator

A child's hand in yours—what tenderness and power it arouses. You are instantly the very touchstone of wisdom and strength.

Marjorie Holmes (1910 - 2002)
American writer, columnist and teacher

Life can only be understood backwards, but it must be lived forwards.

Soren A. Kierkegaard (1813 - 1855)
Danish philosopher and writer

Grandchildren are a renewal of life,
a little bit of us going into the future.

Helene Schellenberg Barnhart
American Author

The birth of a grandchild is like the arrival of Spring, awakening from a deep Winter's sleep and budding forth with new life, bringing joy and optimism for the future.

Vera Allen-Smith

© Peter Weimann / AnimalsAnimals, Roe Deer

A grandchild is a breath of spring on a winter's day—a little flower poking through the snow.

Marilyn Ransom
Grandmother of the late Joseph Kendrick Ransom, 5-day-old organ donor,
from Mrs. Ransom's poem "A Grandchild"

It is not a slight thing when they,
who are so fresh from God, love us.

Charles Dickens (1812 - 1870)
English novelist

© ZSSD / Minden Pictures, Red River Hogs

If becoming a grandmother was only a matter of choice, I should advise every one of you straight away to become one. There is no fun for old people like it!

Hannah Whitall Smith (1832 - 1911)
American evangelist, reformer,
suffragist and author

Perfect love sometimes does not come until the first grandchild.

Welsh proverb

just GRANDPARENTS

WHEN A CHILD IS BORN, SO ARE THE GRANDPARENTS

COMPILED BY BONNIE LOUISE KUCHLER

Published by Willow Creek Press
P.O. Box 147, Minocqua, Wisconsin 54548

Editor/Design: Andrea Donner

Library of Congress Cataloging-in-Publication Data

Just grandparents / compiled by Bonnie Louise Kuchler.
p. cm.
ISBN 1-59543-058-X (hardcover : alk. paper)
1. Grandparents--Quotations. 2. Grandparent and child--Quotations, maxims, etc. I. Kuchler, Bonnie Louise, 1958-
PN6084.G6J87 2004
306.874'5--dc22

2004009887

Printed in Canada

© Barbara Wright / AnimalsAnimals, Miniature Donkeys

Babies are such a nice way to start people.

Don Herold (1889 - 1966)
American author and humorist

© Martin Harvey / Peter Arnold Inc., Chimpanzees

There are 152 distinctly different ways of holding a baby, and they are all right.

Heywood Hale Broun (1918 - 2001)
American broadcast journalist, actor and author

Few things are more delightful than grandchildren fighting over your lap.

Doug Larson
American cartoonist

© Gerard Lacz / AnimalsAnimals, Meercats

Becoming a grandmother is wonderful. One moment you're just a mother. The next you are all-wise and prehistoric.

Pam Brown
American author

Wisdom doesn't necessarily come with age. Sometimes age just shows up all by itself.

Tom Wilson
American cartoonist

They tell you that you'll lose your mind when you grow older. What they don't tell you is that you won't miss it very much.

Malcolm Cowley (1898 - 1989)
American critic and author

© Tui De Roy / Minden Pictures, King Vulture

It is well known that the older a man grows, the faster he could run as a boy.

Red Smith (1905 - 1982)
American sportswriter

Listening children know stories are there. When their elders sit and begin, children are just waiting and hoping for one to come out, like a mouse from a hole.

Eudora Welty (1909 - 2001)
American author

If the very old will remember,
the very young will listen.

Chief Dan George (1899 - 1981)
Actor and Salish chief

Life has loveliness to sell . . .
children's faces looking up
holding wonder like a cup.

Sara Teasdale (1884 – 1933)
American author and poet
from the poem "Barter"

© Johnny Johnson / Alaska Stock, Emperor Penguin

Some of the world's best educators are grandparents.

Dr. Charlie W. Shedd
American minister and author

© Konrad Wothe / Minden Pictures, Pond Slider Turtles

There is so much to teach,
and the time goes so fast.

Erma Bombeck (1927 - 1996)
American journalist, author and humorist

If youth only knew;
if age only could.

Henri Estienne (1531 - 1598)
French scholar and printer

© artwolfe.com, Galapagos Sea Lions

In youth we run into difficulties.
In old age difficulties run into us.

Josh Billings (1818 - 1885)
(pseudonym of Henry Wheeler Shaw)
American humorist

© Gerry Ellis / Minden Pictures, African elephants

You know you're getting old when you stoop to tie your shoes, and wonder what else you can do while you're down there.

George Burns (1896 - 1996)
American actor and comedian

I'm at an age where my back goes out more than I do.

Phyllis Diller (b. 1917)
American comedienne and humanitarian

© Sumio Harada / Minden Pictures, Red Squirrel

Old age is no place for sissies.

Bette Davis (1908 - 1989)
American actress

I *have everything* I *had*
20 *years ago, except now*
it's all lower.

Gypsy Rose Lee (1914 - 1970)
American entertainer

© Wendy Shattil / Bob Rozinski, White Pelican

I refuse to think of them as chin hairs. I think of them as stray eyebrows.

Janette Barber
American writer and producer

Gravity always wins.

Erma Bombeck (1927 - 1996)
American journalist, author and humorist

© Daniel J. Cox / Natural Exposures, Alaskan Brown Bears

*Grandchildren are God's way
of compensating us for growing old.*

Mary H. Waldrip

The young and the old
are closest to life.
They love every minute dearly.

Chief Dan George
Actor and Salish chief

If growing up is the process of creating ideas and dreams about what life should be, then maturity is letting go again.

Mary Beth Danielson
American writer

© Kennan Ward / Bruce Coleman, Inc., Chimpanzees

Being grandparents sufficiently removes us from the responsibilities so that we can be friends.

Dr. Allan Fromme
American author

They say genes skip generations. Maybe that's why grandparents find their grandchildren so likeable.

Joan McIntosh
American author

The best baby-sitters, of course, are the baby's grandparents. You feel completely comfortable entrusting your baby to them for long periods, which is why most grandparents flee to Florida.

Dave Barry (b. 1947)
American columnist and humorist

A *child is a most desirable pest.*

Max Gramlich

The simplest toy, one which even the youngest child can operate, is called a grandparent.

Sam Levenson (1911 – 1980)
American humorist and author

*If nothing is going well,
call your grandmother.*

Italian Proverb

© Budd Titlow / Naturegraphs, Longbilled Marsh Wren

Nobody can do for little children what grandparents do. Grandparents sort of sprinkle stardust over the lives of little children.

Alex Haley (1921 - 1992)
American novelist and journalist

© Steve Bloom / stevebloom.com, Giraffes

Grandmas are moms
with lots of frosting.

Author Unknown

What children need most are the essentials that grandparents provide in abundance. They give unconditional love, kindness, patience, humor, comfort, lessons in life. And, most importantly, cookies.

Rudolph W. Giuliani
Mayor of New York City

© Frans Lanting / Minden Pictures, White Tern

Youth is like spring, an over-praised season . . . more remarkable, as a general rule, for biting east winds than genial breezes. Autumn is the mellower season, and what we lose in flowers we more than gain in fruits.

Samuel Butler (1835 - 1902)
English writer and poet

© artwolfe.com, Gray Wolf

*We are only young once.
That is all society can stand.*

Bob Bowen
American bassist

Beautiful young people are accidents of nature, but beautiful old people are works of art.

Eleanor Roosevelt (1884 - 1962) (attributed)
American humanitarian and diplomat

© artwolfe.com, Mute Swan

As we grow old, the beauty steals inward.

Ralph Waldo Emerson (1803 - 1882)
American essayist and poet

© Steve Bloom / stevebloom.com, Japanese Macaque

To know how to grow old is the master-work of wisdom, and one of the most difficult chapters in the great art of living.

Henri-Frederic Amiel (1821 - 1881)
Swiss philosopher, critic and writer

To keep the heart unwrinkled,
to be hopeful, kindly,
cheerful, reverent—that is
to triumph over old age.

Thomas Bailey Aldrich (1836 - 1907)
American novelist

Life is no brief candle to me.
It's sort of a splendid torch which
I've got to hold up for the moment,
and I want to make it burn
as brightly as possible before handing
it on to future generations.

George Bernard Shaw (1856 – 1950)
Irish dramatist, novelist and critic

© artwolfe.com, Guanaco & Chulengo

And in the end, it's not the years in your life that count. It's the life in your years.

Abraham Lincoln (1809 - 1865)
16th president of the U. S.

© Ron Kimball / ronkimballstock.com, Hippopotamus

Bibliography

Grateful acknowledgment is made to the authors and publishers for use of the following material. If notified, the publisher will be pleased to rectify an omission in future editions.

Baker, Brian. (2001) "QuoteWorld.org – Over 15,000 Quotations and Famous Quotes." http://www.quoteworld.org [accessed 24 February 2004].

Barry, Dave. *Babies and Other Hazards of Sex: How to Make a Tiny Person in Only 9 Months, with Tools You Probably Have around the Home*. New York: Rodale Press, 2000.

Booth, Carolyn J. and Mindy B. Henderson. *Grandparents: Gifts of Love, Humor and Wisdom*. Nashville: Rutledge Hill Press (A Thomas Nelson Company), 2000.

Butler, Samuel. *The Way of All Flesh*. New York: Modern Library (a registered Trademark of Random House), 1998.

Cohen, Gene D., M.D., Ph.D. *The Creative Age: Awakening Human Potential in the Second Half of Life*. New York: Avon Books (an imprint of HarperCollins Publishers), 2000.

Cotner, June, ed. *Bless the Day: Prayers & Poems to Nurture Your Soul*. New York: Kodansha America, 1998.

Covey, Stephen R. *First Things First: To Live, to Love, to Learn, to Leave a Legacy* New York: Fireside (trademark of Simon & Schuster), 1995.

Danielson, Mary Beth, et al. *Reinventing Home: Six Working Women Look at Their Home Lives.* New York: Plume, 1991.

DeFord, Deborah, ed. *Reader's Digest Quotable Quotes: Wit and Wisdom for all Occasions from America's Most Popular Magazine.* Pleasantville, NY: The Reader's Digest Association, 1997.

Diller, Phyllis. *The Joys of Aging—And How to Avoid Them.* New York: Doubleday, 1981.

Fletcher, Jim and Roger Howerton, ed. *The Joyous Gift of Grandparents.* Green Forest, AR: New Leaf Press, 2003.

George, Chief Dan. *My Heart Soars.* Surrey, British Columbia: Hancock House Publishers, 1989.

Klein, Allen. *Up Words for Down Days.* New York: Gramercy Books (an imprint of Random House), 1998.

Lanese, Janet. *Grandmothers Are Like Snowflakes . . . No Two are Alike: Words of Wisdom, Gentle Advice, and Hilarious Observations.* New York: Dell Publishing, 1996.

Lanese, Janet. *More Grandmothers Are Like Snowflakes...No Two Are Alike: A Treasury of Wit, Wisdom, and Heartwarming Observations.* New York: Delacorte Press (Random House), 2002.

Levenson, Sam. *You Don't Have to Be in "Who's Who" to Know What's What.* New York: Simon & Schuster, 1979.

Mead, Lucy. *Grandparents are Special: A Tribute to Those Who Love, Nurture & Inspire.* New York: Gramercy Books (an imprint of Random House), 2000.

Mindeman, Miriam and Annette LaPlaca, comp. *A Truly Spectacular, Terrific, Fabulous, Awesome, Remarkable Grandparent.* Wheaton, IL: Harold Shaw Publishers, 1997.

Phillips, Bob. *Phillips' Book of Great Thoughts and Funny Sayings.* Wheaton, IL: Tyndale House Publishers, 1993.

Roosevelt, David B. *Grandmere: A Personal History of Eleanor Roosevelt.* New York: Warner Books, 2002.

Turkington, Carol A. *The Quotable Woman: Words of Wisdom from Mother Teresa, Katherine Hepburn, Edith Wharton, Oprah Winfrey, Virginia Woolf, and More.* New York: McGraw-Hill, 2000.

Unknown author. *365 Daily Thoughts & Inspirations about Grandmothers.* Cypress, CA: Avalanche Publishing, 2003.